THE
WEST HAM UTD
COLLECTION

DB
PUBLISHING

First published in Great Britain in 2003 by
The Breedon Books Publishing Company Limited
Breedon House, 3 The Parker Centre,
Derby, DE21 4SZ.

This edition published in Great Britain in 2012 by
The Derby Books Publishing Company Limited,
3 The Parker Centre, Derby, DE21 4SZ.

ISBN 978-1-78091-135-9

Printed and bound by Copytech (UK) Limited, Peterborough.

Contents

Introduction

I N 1895, workers at the Thames Ironworks, which was situated at the mouth of the River Lea in East London, decided to form a football team. It was an instant success. Players were easy to recruit, spectators were eager to watch their matches – so much so that a crowd of 3,000 turned up to see the club's first-ever FA Cup match the same year – and a legend was born.

Soon the club was playing in the highly competitive Southern League.

Five years after the club's formation, Thames Ironworks FC was wound up – and almost immediately relaunched as West Ham United FC, who went straight into the Southern League to take the place vacated by their predecessors. The reason for the change, of course, was that the club wanted to introduce professionalism, which did not sit easily with a works side.

In 1904 the Hammers moved to their present home, the Boleyn Ground at Upton Park, and in the first season after World War One they were elected to the Football League. Their first League game was on 30 August 1919, when they drew 1-1 with Lincoln City at home.

In 1923 the Hammers were promoted to the top flight as runners-up in the Second Division. The same season they took part in one of the most historic football matches in the game's long story – the first FA Cup Final to be held at Wembley.

The Hammers retained their place in the old First Division until 1932 and it was to prove a difficult task to return. Not until 1958 did West Ham United again play in the top flight of English football, although they did win the League's War Cup at Wembley in 1940.

Once back in the First Division the Hammers stayed there for 20 years and in that time won major honours for the first time. Indeed, these were golden days: FA Cup Final victories in 1964 and 1975 and the European Cup-winners' Cup in 1965. And even as a Second Division club again in 1980, the Hammers lifted the FA Cup again.

This book covers the years from the fledgling West Ham United in the early years of the 20th century, up to that third FA Cup Final victory, all the more sweet because it was at the expense of London rivals, Arsenal.

Hammers fans turning these pages will relive great days in their club's story. It will revive memories for those who were there, and inform and entertain those who have only read about the Hammers' moments of glory.

Early Days

Plymouth Argyle goalkeeper Pinnell punches clear from a West Ham attack at the Memorial Grounds, Canning Town, in January 1904. A crowd of 8,000 saw a 1-1 draw. The Memorial Grounds were opened in 1897 and named to commemorate the 60th year of Queen Victoria's reign. There were facilities for cycling, football and athletics and the stadium could accommodate 100,000. It was nominated for a possible replay of the 1901 FA Cup Final between Spurs and West Brom.

West Ham United in 1904-05, when they finished 11th in the Southern League. Back row (left to right): Herbert Bamlett, Aubrey Fair, Matt Kingsley, Dave Gardner, Syd King (secretary-manager). Middle row: T. Robinson (trainer), Fred Brunton, Tommy Allison, Frank Piercy, John Russell, Len Jarvis, Fred Mercer, Charlie Paynter (assistant trainer). Front row: William McCartney, Charlie Simmons, Billy Bridgman, Jack Fletcher, Chris Carrick, Jack Flynn.

The Boleyn Ground pictured in 1905, a far cry from the stadium of the 21st century.

West Ham United, 1905-06, a season in which the Hammers again finished 11th in the Southern League. Back row (left to right): Syd Hammond, Alex McCartney, George Kitchen, Charlie Cotton, Dave Gardner. Middle row: W. White, Syd King (secretary-manager), Tommy Allison, Harry Hindle, Frank Piercy, T. Robinson (trainer), Charlie Paynter (assistant trainer). Front row: William Ford, Herbert Winterhalder, S. McAllister, Charlie Mackie, George Hilsdon, Billy Bridgeman, H. Wilkinson, Lionel Watson, Fred Blackburn, Arthur Winterhalder.

On the first day of the 1906-07 Southern League season – 1 September – temperatures topped 90 degrees. In the sweltering heat at White Hart Lane, West Ham beat Spurs 2-1.

More action from the game against Tottenham

Hammers regular goalkeeper in their Southern League days was George Kitchen, who was also a professional golfer. He joined West Ham from Everton in September 1905 – and scored a goal, hitting home a penalty against Swindon Town. Kitchen overcame a serious injury in 1908 to take his career with the Hammers to 205 League and Cup games, and six goals. He moved to Southampton in 1911 and had two more seasons there before becoming a golf professional in Bournemouth.

West Ham United in 1907-08. The Hammers finished tenth in the Southern League. Back row (left to right): Syd Hammond, William Wildman, David Clarke, George Kitchen, Charlie Simmons, A. Taylor, James Gault. Middle row: T. Robinson (trainer), Daniel Woodards, Tommy Allison, Frank Piercy, Syd King (secretary-manager), Len Jarvis, Robert Young, George Horn, Charlie Paynter (assistant trainer). Seated: David Lindsay, Tom Randall, William Brown, A.Reed, Billy Grassam, Harry Stapley, Alf Harwood, Lionel Watson, Fred Blackburn, Tom Lee. On ground: Arthur Featherstone, Fred Kemp.

West Ham United in 1909-10. Back row (left to right): Syd Hammond, Fred Shreeve, Harold Dawson, George Kitchen, Robert Fairman, W. Bourne. Middle row: Charlie Paynter (assistant trainer), Robert Whiteman, Stanley, William Lavery, Daniel Woodards, Syd King (secretary-manager), George Wagstaffe, Frank Piercy, Tom Randall, Rist, T. Robinson (trainer). Front row: Armstrong, Herbert Ashton, Danny Shea, Frank Cannon, George Webb, W.F.White (chairman), Vincent Haynes, Carvossa, David Waggott, Fred Blackburn, Tom Caldwell, William Silor.

Danny Shea came from Wapping and when he made his Southern League debut for West Ham in 1907-08 he was still an amateur. When he moved to Blackburn halfway through the 1912-13 season he had scored 121 goals in 201 League and Cup games for West Ham.

Syd Puddefoot joined West Ham from East London junior football in 1912-13 and stayed until 1922, when he surprisingly moved to Scotland to play for Falkirk. He rejoined the Hammers in 1932, now aged 36 and after a successful career with Blackburn, but could not help West Ham in their battle to avoid relegation to Division Two. He ended his playing days in 1932-33. For the Hammers Puddefoot had scored 107 goals in 194 peacetime games and had also been a prolific scorer in wartime football. At Blackburn he won two England caps and an FA Cup winners' medal.

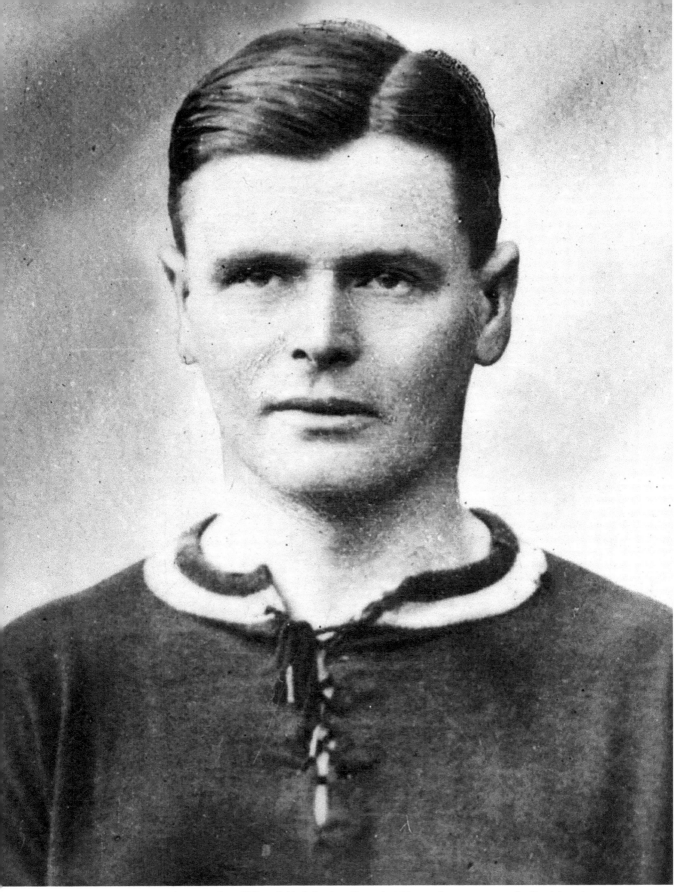

Full-back William Cope joined the Hammers from Oldham Athletic in 1914. He made 147 peacetime appearances for the club and many more during the war. Cope was transferred to Wrexham in 1922, when he was 36.

In the first round of the 1913-14 FA Cup, the Hammers beat Chesterfield 8-1 at Upton Park. Syd Puddefoot scored five of the West Ham goals including a hat-trick in only seven minutes. Here, the Derbyshire side are under pressure yet again.Chesterfield were then a non-League club, having failed to gain re-election in 1909.

The White Horse Cup Final

West Ham in April 1923, on the brink of their historic FA Cup Final at Wembley, the first at the new stadium. Back row (left to right): Syd King (manager), Billy Henderson, Syd Bishop, George Kay, Ted Hufton, John Young, Jack Tresadern, Charlie Paynter (trainer). Front row: Dick Richards, Billy Brown, Vic Watson, Billy Moore, Jimmy Ruffell.

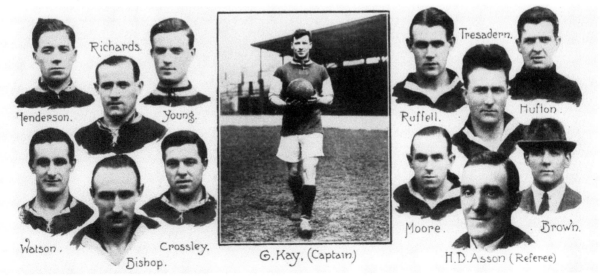

How one magazine pictured West Ham's 1923 FA Cup Final team. Dick Crossley was the unlucky man who did not play. Referee H.D. Asson of West Bromwich has also got in on the picture.

West Ham supporters arrive at Wembley for the 1923 FA Cup Final apparently unaware of the huge crush they would soon encounter.

Crowds swarm towards the Wembley turnstiles as a huge crowd builds up to take the authorities completely by surprise. Not surprisingly, all future FA Cup Finals would be all-ticket affairs.

The huge crowd at Wembley Stadium for the 1923 FA Cup Final between the Hammers and Bolton Wanderers. The official attendance was 126,047 – 90,520 through the turnstiles and 35,527 advance ticket holders – but it is probable that up to 200,000 people were at the stadium. The gross receipts for the first Wembley Final were £27,776.

Fans were still clambering into Wembley well after the closing of the turnstiles.

Yet more would-spectators climb over the stadium walls, most of them dressed as if they were off to work for the day.

This fan seemed intent on getting into the game, even if it meant risking his life.

PC Storey, on his white horse Billy, attempts to push the crowd back. Of course there were many other police horses helping out in the stadium but because Billy was so noticeable he entered football folklore as the horse who did it all by himself.

Other mounted officers attempt to hold the Wembley crowd in check.

West Ham's players look perplexed as the police try to clear the pitch.

What to do next? Police officers chat to the crowd whilst two fans take a stroll across the pitch.

The game finally under way, West Ham's Billy Moore collects a pass from Jimmy Ruffell.

Only three minutes gone and Bolton's David Jack scores one of the most historic goals in football history – the first ever in a Wembley FA Cup Final. Eight minutes into the second half, Bolton scored again and the Cup was theirs.

This time Jack is beaten to the ball by the West Ham defence.

Heads high in the Bolton defence as the Hammers mount another attack.

The Twenties and Thirties

West Ham's first manager Syd King (left) held the job from 1902 until 1932. His assistant Charlie Paynter (right) took over until 1950. Thus the Hammers had only two managers in 48 years.

West Ham on the attack against Bolton at Upton Park in December 1923, a game which the Hammers lost 1-0. The previous week the sides had drawn 1-1 at Burnden Park.

Vivian Gibbins was one of the last amateurs to play for England in a full international. He enjoyed a good scoring rate with the Hammers – 63 goals in 138 senior games – whom he joined from Clapton in 1923. His amateur career often meant he was absent for the Hammers. His last game was in 1931-32, after which he played for Brentford, Bristol Rovers and Southampton.

Wing-half Jack Tresadern joined West Ham in 1913 from East London junior football. He won a regular first-team place after World War One and stayed until 1924 when Burnley signed him. Tresadern, who was capped twice for England, appeared in 166 League and FA Cup games for the Hammers, scoring five goals.

January 1924 and Third Division South side Aberdare Athletic are overwhelmed 5-0 in the first round of the FA Cup.

George Kay has just scored for the Hammers against Leeds United in the second round of the FA Cup in January 1924. The sides drew 1-1 but Leeds won the Elland Road replay 1-0.

George Kay was centre-half and captain of West Ham's 1923 FA Cup Final team which lost to Bolton Wanderers, the club Kay had rejected in 1911. Kay joined the Hammers from Irish football in 1919 and when he left for Stockport in 1926 he had made 259 senior appearances for West Ham, scoring 17 goals.

Inside-forward Billy Moore had been capped by England in amateur internationals before he joined West Ham from Sunderland in the 1922 close season. His first season was remarkable and as the Hammers were promoted and reached the FA Cup Final, Moore played in every game, scoring 20 goals. He was capped once by England – and scored twice – and when he retired in 1928-29 had scored 48 goals in 202 senior appearances for West Ham. He served on the club's coaching staff until 1960.

Goalkeeper Ted Hufton made his League debut for the Hammers in the first season after World War One and altogether appeared in 401 League and FA Cup games before leaving Upton Park for Watford in 1933. In one two-season spell Hufton, who was capped six times for England, saved 11 of the 18 penalties he faced for the Hammers.

Billy Henderson joined West Ham from Aberdare Athletic in 1922. A full-back, he made 183 first-team appearances before leaving Upton Park in 1928. Six years later he was dead, from tuberculosis.

The opening day of the 1925-26 season – the first under the new offside law – and a Hammers player struggles to keep possession as two Manchester United players try to get to the ball. Stan Earle won the game for the Hammers, 1-0, but they could only finish 18th in the First Division.

In the third round of the FA Cup in January 1926, the Hammers were themselves hammered, 5-0, by Tottenham at White Hart Lane. In a rare West Ham attack the Spurs' goalkeeper Bill Kaine dives at the feet of Vic Watson.

Syd Bishop, a versatile half-back or inside-forward who made 172 League and FA Cup appearances for the Hammers after signing from Ilford just after World War One. He went to Leicester City in 1926 and later enjoyed a good career with Chelsea. Bishop was capped four times for England after he left Upton Park.

Jack Hebden was a dependable full-back who joined West Ham from Bradford City in 1921. In 1928 he moved to Fulham with another Hammers full-back, Gorge Horler, for £850, after 116 senior appearances for West Ham.

Ted Hufton rushes out to clear with his feet against Aston Villa at Upton Park in September 1928. The Hammers won 4-1.

West Ham goalkeeper David Baillie attempts to block a shot from Liverpool's Jimmy McDougall at Upton Park in October 1928 but the ball found its way into the net.

Ted Hufton punches clear from a Derby County forward at Upton Park in late September 1929. The Hammers won 2-0 to inflict upon Derby their first defeat of the season

The Hammers clear another Derby attack The Rams went on to finish runners-up in the old First Division, the Hammers seventh.

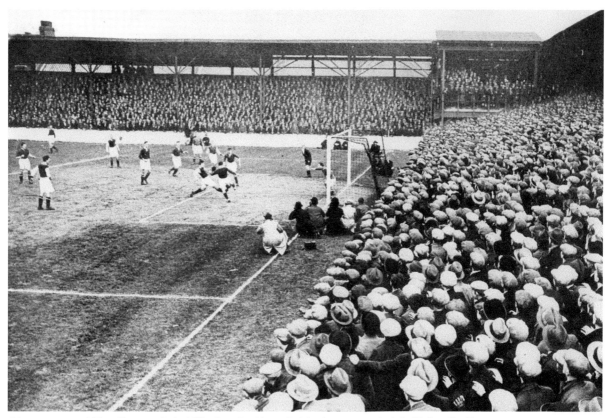

February 1930 and West Ham attack the Millwall goal at Upton Park in the fifth round of the FA Cup. The Hammers won 4-1.

West Ham defend a corner against Arsenal during the quarter-final FA Cup match at Highbury in March 1930. The Gunners won 3-0.

Hammers goalkeeper Ted Hufton managed to parry this shot but the Gunners were not to be denied for long.

Manchester City visited Upton Park in 1930-31 and City's Bobby Marshall slips, much to the relief of goalkeeper Bob Dixon and defenders Jimmy Collins and Alf Earl.

Vic Watson holds several records for West Ham: 298 League goals in his career; 42 League goals in a season (1929-30); six goals in one game (against Leeds in February 1929). Altogether he hit 326 goals in 505 League and FA Cup games for the Hammers. He joined West Ham in 1920, from Cambridgeshire non-League football, and had one season with Southampton before retiring in 1936. Watson was capped five times for England.

Vivien Gibbins watches his shot go wide against Aston Villa at Upton Park in January 1931. Gibbins, however, went on to score twice in a 5-5 draw.

This time Gibbins (far left) watches his shot on its way into the Villa net in the ten-goal thriller.

Hammers fans in good spirits at Stamford Bridge for the FA Cup fourth-round game against Chelsea in January 1932. Alas, the visitors lost 3-1.

Hughie Gallacher of Chelsea and West Ham's Alf Chalkley and Jim Barrett are all airborne.

West Brom goalkeeper Pearson grabs the ball from the Hammers' Arthur Wilson in the FA Cup fourth-round match at Upton Park in January 1933.

Brighton's defenders can do nothing but look dismayed after Jackie Morton's winner in the FA Cup fifth-round replay at Upton Park in February 1933.

The Hammers went on to the FA Cup semi-final in 1933, where they lost 2-1 to Everton at Molineux Here the Hammers' goalkeeper George Watson cannot stop Dunn's header.

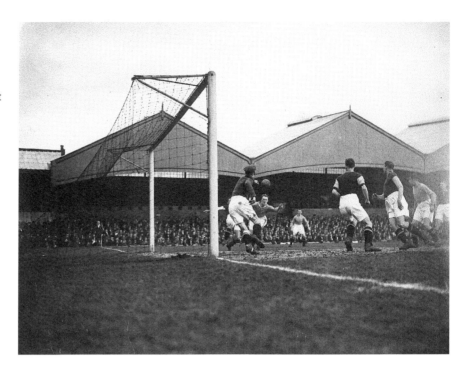

West Ham goalkeeper George Watson chases the ball during the 1933 FA Cup semi-final against Everton at Molineux. Another Watson – Vic – scored for the Hammers.

Jimmy Ruffell takes on Stockport County goalkeeper Frank McDonough at Edgeley Park in January 1935. West Ham surprisingly lost this FA Cup third-round replay 1-0 to the Third Division North side.

A Bradford Park Avenue defender gets in a tackle on West Ham's Jackie Morton at Upton Park in September 1937. The Hammers won the Second Division match 3-1.

West Ham United, 1937-38. Back row (left to right): Charlie Bicknell, Benny Fenton, Norman Corbett, Jack Weare, Richard Walker, Charlie Walker. Front row: Stan Foxall, Archie Macaulay, Sam Small, Len Goulden, Joe Cockcroft, John Morton. At the end of the season the Hammers were ninth in Division Two.

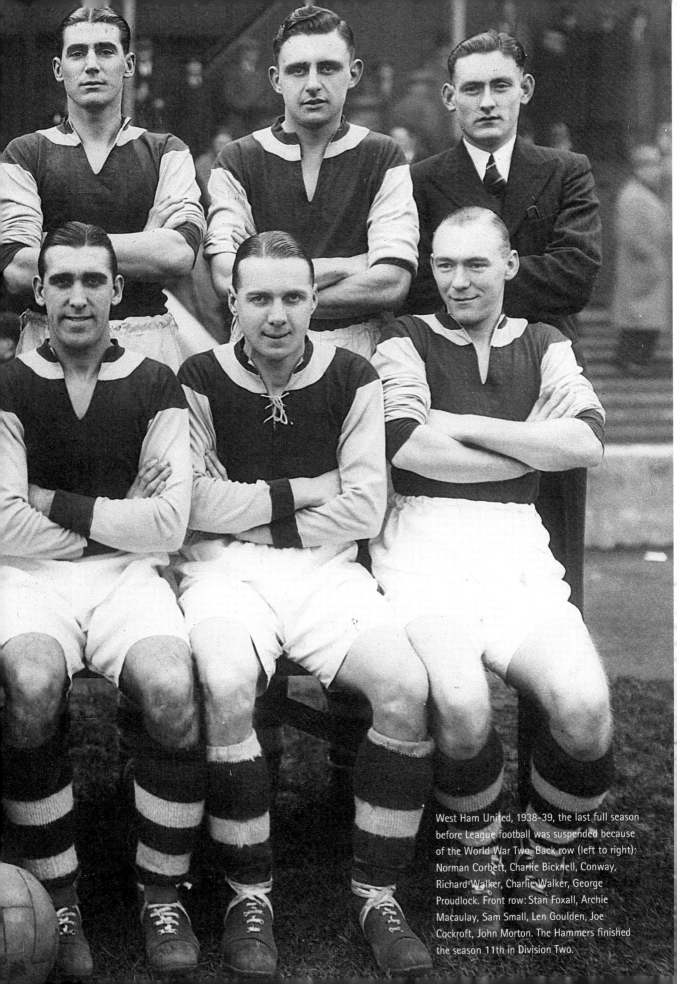

West Ham United, 1938-39, the last full season before League football was suspended because of the World War Two. Back row (left to right): Norman Corbett, Charlie Bicknell, Conway, Richard Walker, Charlie Walker, George Proudlock. Front row: Stan Foxall, Archie Macaulay, Sam Small, Len Goulden, Joe Cockroft, John Morton. The Hammers finished the season 11th in Division Two.

West Ham's Archie Macaulay scores the winner against Spurs at Highbury in the fourth-round second FA Cup replay in February 1939. The Hammers went out 2-0 at Portsmouth in the quarter-final.

A crowd of 13,400, many of them in uniform, watched the last League game at Upton Park before World War Two. The Hammers lost 2-0 to Leicester City on 2 September 1939. The following day Prime Minister Neville Chamberlain made his fateful wireless broadcast.

In June 1940, invasion scares were put to the back of supporters' minds – for 90 minutes at least – when the Hammers met Blackburn Rovers in the Final of the Football League War Cup at Wembley. West Ham lifted the trophy 1-0, thanks to a 34th-minute winner from Sam Small. These photographs show action from the game.

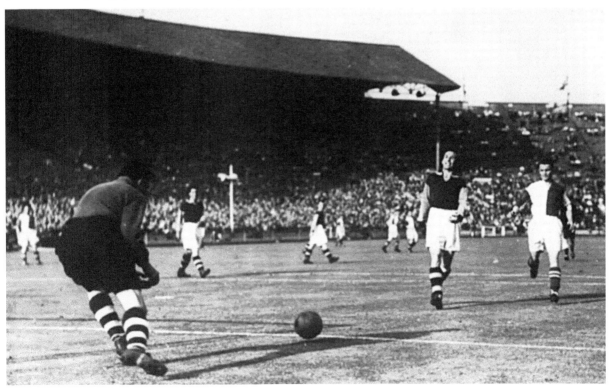

The Post-War Years

Hammers centre-forward Bill Robinson challenges Tottenham goalkeeper Ted Ditchburn in the 1-1 draw at White Hart Lane in February 1949.

West Ham manager Ted Fenton and his team at their snowbound training headquarters at Letchworth before the 1953 FA Cup third-round tie against West Brom. This special trip did not work, alas, as the Hammers went down 4-1.

Harry Hooper (falling) scores the Hammers' second goal against Huddersfield Town at Upton Park in the FA Cup third-round game in January 1954. Len Quested and Don McAvoy are the Huddersfield players.

In the 1953-54 FA Cup, the Hammers lost to holders Blackpool at Bloomfield Road in a fourth-round replay. This is the first game at Upton Park, where Hammers goalkeeper Ernie Gregory grabs at the ball in a crowded goalmouth.

Dave Sexton gets the better of Bristol Rovers' long-serving centre-half Ray Warren at Upton Park in September 1954. Sexton scored in the Hammers' 5-2 win.

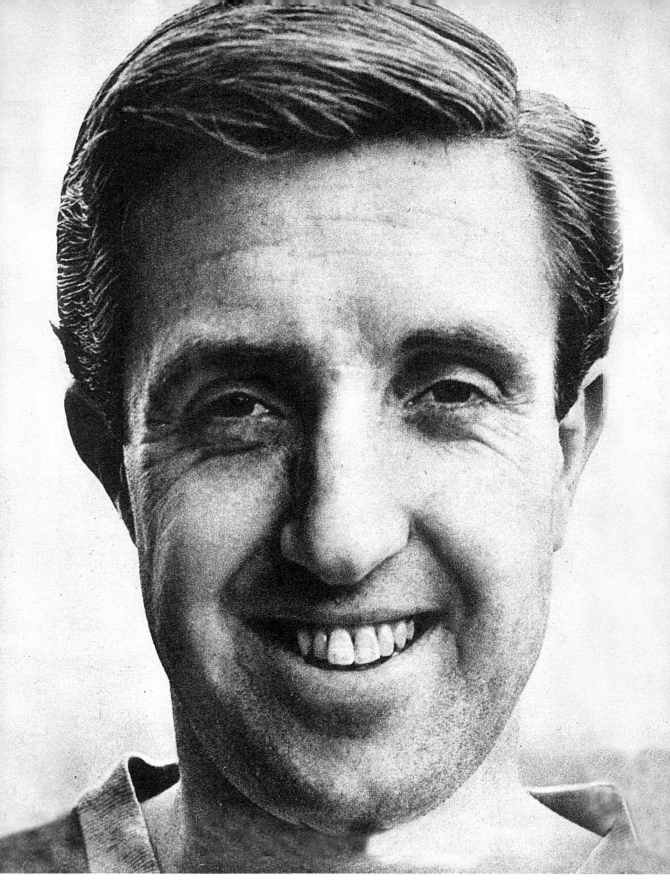

John Bond was another ex-Hammer of the 1950s who found a new career as a manager. Bond, a full-back, signed from non-League Colchester United and went on to make 428 senior appearances for West Ham, scoring 35 goals, before becoming a Torquay United player in 1966. He was a mainstay of the 1957-58 promotion side. Bond managed several clubs including Norwich and Manchester City.

Malcolm Allison signed for the Hammers from Charlton Athletic in 1951 and played 255 League and FA Cup games at centre-half. Allison, like so many of his Hammers teammates of the 1950s, had a fine tactical brain. Alas, he lost a lung because of tuberculosis and never played for the Hammers in the top flight. One of the game's most colourful characters, he went into management, most famously with Joe Mercer at Manchester City.

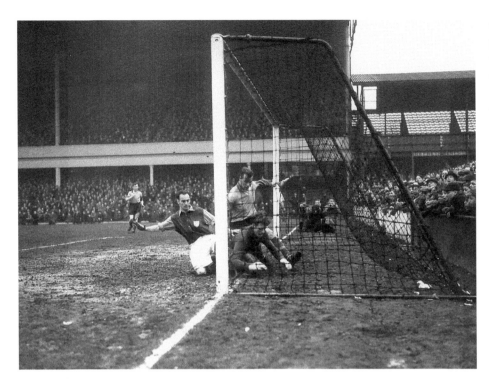

West Ham's Albert Foan beats John Charles and Ray Wood of Leeds to score the winner at Upton Park in March 1955. The Hammers triumphed 2-1.

West Ham in 1955-56. Back row (left to right): Dave Sexton, John Bond, Ernie Gregory, Malcolm Allison, Noel Cantwell, Frank O"Farrell. Front row: Malcolm Musgrove, Harry Hooper, Billy Dare, John Dick, Ken Tucker.

Only three players have scored more goals for West Ham than John Dick, who netted 166 in 351 League and Cup games between 1953-54 and 1962-63. He signed in 1953, from non-League football, and 1962 was transferred to Brentford. In his second season at Upton Park, Dick equalled the club's post-war record of 26 League goals in a season. He was capped once for Scotland.

January 1956 and Hammers manager Ted Fenton gives the team a tactics talk at Hove greyhound racing track before the FA cup fourth-round game against Cardiff City in January 1956. This time 'special' Cup training seems to have worked because West Ham won 2-1.

John Dick scores West Ham's second goal – and one of his hat-trick – against Spurs with a back header. This FA Cup sixth-round game ended 3-3 at White Hart Lane in March 1956 but Tottenham won the Upton Park replay 2-1.

Those Golden Years

West Ham United, 1955-56. Back row (left to right): Andy Malcolm, George Wright, George Taylor, Les Bennett, Noel Cantwell, Frank O'Farrell. Front row: Roy Stroud, Brian Moore, Billy Dare, John Dick, Malcolm Musgrove, Malcolm Allison. The Hammers finished the season 16th in Division Two.

West Ham skipper Malcolm Allison leads out the Hammers in March 1956.

Liverpool goalkeeper Dick Rudham gets in a tangle with John Dick at Upton Park in April 1958. The sides drew 1-1 and after a 3-1 win at Ayresome Park the following week, the Hammers were back in the top flight.

West Ham on the eve of 1958-59, their first season back in the top flight. From top to bottom are: Ernie Gregory, John Bond, Malcolm Pyke, Andy Nelson, Vic Keeble, Noel Cantwell, John Dick, Ken Brown, Bill Lansdowne, Andy Malcolm, Mike Grice, Malcolm Musgrove, John Smith and Billy Dare.

Centre-half Ken Brown made 455 senior appearances for the Hammers, making his debut in 1952-53 and remaining at Upton Park until 1966-67. He took over from Malcolm Allison and was a key member of the 1957-58 promotion team.

Arsenal's Vic Groves scores against the Hammers at Highbury in November 1959 but West Ham were the winners, 3-1.

West Ham goalkeeper Noel Cantwell makes a spectacular save from Nottingham Forest's Scottish international Stewart Imlach in the 4-1 Hammers win at Upton Park in December 1959.

West Ham's Ken Brown and the Fulham amateur international R.H. Brown in action at Craven Cottage in October 1960 when the London rivals fought out a 1-1 draw.

Hammers goalkeeper Brian Rhodes dives at the feet of Arsenal's David Herd at Highbury in March 1961. The result was a goalless draw.

Goalkeeper Lawrie Leslie grabs the ball as Geoff Hurst covers his West Ham colleague at Upton Park in September 1961. The Hammers beat Leicester City 3-1.

Ted Fenton had been the Hammers manager for 11 years when he left Upton Park in 1961, in circumstances that have never been properly explained. The board issued a statement saying that he was suffering from 'strain' and was on sick leave. A former Hammers player, Fenton, whose greatest achievement was to take the club back into the top flight in 1958, became manager of Southend United.

Ron Greenwood, who had appeared in Chelsea's League championship team of 1954-55 as well as playing for Bradford, Brentford and Fulham, was the first manager of West Ham who had not played for the Hammers. He was appointed in April 1961, after coaching at Arsenal and with the England Under-23 team. The Greenwood era was the most successful in the club's history, culminating in European glory in 1965. He was appointed general manager in 1974, when former player John Lyall was made team manager, and after Don Revie's shock departure, Greenwood was England's manager for five years.

This time Leslie hurls himself at Fulham's Graham Leggatt but it was the Cottagers' forward who got his side's second goal at Craven Cottage in October 1961, when the Hammers went down 2-0. The other players, left to right, are Dave Metchick of Fulham and West Ham's Joe Kirkup (2) and John Bond.

Lawrie Leslie punches clear from Arsenal's Alan Skirton at Highbury in December 1961.The game ended in a 2-2 draw.

Bobby Moore and Chelsea's Colin Shaw in a heading duel at Stamford Bridge in February 1962. Moore scored the only goal of the game.

Peter Brabrook was born not far from Upton Park and supported the Hammers as a boy, but he cost them £35,000 when he signed from Chelsea in October 1962. He went on to net 43 goals in 214 games before moving to Orient in 1968. Tall for a winger, Brabrook played for England in the 1958 World Cup finals.

West Ham's Johnny Byrne challenges Arsenal goalkeeper John McClelland at Highbury in October 1962. The game ended 1-1.

Johnny Byrne enjoyed a remarkable strike rate for West Ham – 107 goals in 205 League, Cup and European games. When he was with Crystal Palace he was the first player from the Fourth Division to win a full England cap. Byrne joined the Hammers in 1962 for £45,000 and returned to Selhurst Park in 1967, for £65,000. He was capped 11 times at full level.

Full-back Joe Kirkup was another product of the Hammers' youth policy. He played in the 1957 FA Youth Cup Final against Manchester United and made his League debut against Manchester City in 1958. He won England Under-23 caps and played in the 1965 Cup-winners' Cup Final before moving to Chelsea the following year.

Welsh international winger Phil Woosnam had a university degree when West Ham signed him from Leyton Orient for £30,000 in 1958. He made 147 League and Cup appearances, scoring 27 goals, before moving to Aston Villa in 1963. Woosnam later emigrated and was a key figure in setting up the North American Soccer League.

Ken Brown beats Aston Villa's colourful Irish striker Derek Dougan at Upton Park in the 1-1 draw between the sides in December 1962.

Jim Burkett gets in a tackle but Everton's Alex Young manages to cross the ball at Upton Park in March 1963, when the Hammers won 1-0 in the fifth round of the FA Cup.

More from the Cup tie in 1963, this time Ken Brown is involved in an aerial battle with Everton goalkeeper Gordon West.

West Ham's Martin Peters gets the ball away from Roger Hunt as the Hammers' goalkeeper Jim Standen rushes out at Anfield in September 1963. Hunt scored in the game but the Hammers won 2-1.

Martin Peters and Aston Villa's Ron Wylie get in an aerial tangle at Villa Park in October 1963, in the third round of the League Cup. The Hammers won 2-0 and went on to reach the semi-final where they went out to Leicester City.

Goalkeeper Jim Standen made 235 senior appearances for West Ham, for whom he signed in 1962 from Luton Town after earlier appearing 35 times for Arsenal. Standen, who was also a first-class cricketer with Worcestershire – he helped them win the County Championship – moved to Millwall in 1968.

Johnny Byrne scrambles the ball into the net for West Ham's second goal against Blackburn Rovers at Upton Park on Boxing Day 1963. The Hammers scored twice all right, but Blackburn replied with eight to inflict upon them the heaviest home defeat in West Ham's history. Two days later, the Hammers won 3-1 at Ewood Park.

A real tangle on the West Ham goal-line in the 1964 FA Cup Final against Preston North End. Bobby Moore (6) and goalkeeper Jim Standen are on the line with Preston's Alec Ashworth, while Ken Brown and North End's Alex Dawson look on. Happily for the Hammers the ball finished up on top of their net.

Eight minutes into the second half of the 1964 FA Cup Final, Geoff Hurst (on knees) watches his header rebound off the Preston bar and into the net for the equalising goal.

Ronnie Boyce celebrates his injury-time winning goal to give West Ham the Cup. Johnny Byrne (left of picture) joins in.

Bobby Moore holds aloft the FA Cup after the Hammers' 3-2 Wembley victory over Preston North End.

West Ham United bring the FA Cup back home to the East End in 1964.

Bobby Moore (6) and Ken Brown watch Leeds United's Bobby Collins take the ball forward at Elland Road in April 1965.

Ken Brown seems to be caught on the wrong foot as Leeds' Jim Storrie chases the ball. West Ham went down 2-1.

Martin Peters and Dave Bickles in a heading duel with Spurs' Frank Saul at White Hart Lane in April 1966. West Ham won 4-1.

Tireless midfielder Ronnie Boyce made his League debut for West Ham in 1960, when he was only 17 and eventually appeared in 339 senior games, scoring 29 goals, before joining the coaching staff at Upton Park.

Brian Dear watches his effort beat Real Zaragoza goalkeeper Enrique Yarza in the first leg of the 1964-65 European Cup-winners' Cup semi-final at Upton Park in April 1965. The Hammers won 2-1 on the night and eventually took the tie 3-2 on aggregate to set up a Final meeting with TSV Munich at Wembley.

West Ham players admire the 1964-65 European Cup-winners' Cup after their 2-0 Wembley victory over TSV Munich in May 1965.

The Hammers on their night of European glory, celebrating with the Cup-winners' Cup.

The European Cup-winners' Cup team. Back row (left to right): Ken Brown, Martin Peters, Joe Kirkup, Jim Standen, Brian Dear, Bobby Moore. Front row: Alan Sealey, Ronnie Boyce, Geoff Hurst, Jack Burkett and John Sissons.

What a year 1966 was for the Hammers trio Geoff Hurst, Bobby Moore and Martin Peters, seen here with their adoring fans after the World Cup triumph.

Booby Moore shows off the European Cup-winners' Cup at Newham Town Hall, helped by the Mayor, Councillor Terence C. McMillan.

Bobby Moore made 642 first-team appearances for West Ham, a West Ham record at the time, and won a record 108 caps for England. He was the pin-up boy of the 1960s, the man who skippered England to World Cup glory. In both the defence of his club and country, he was supreme. Moore left for Fulham in March 1974 and played against his old club in the following year's FA Cup Final. The football world was shattered when Bobby Moore died from bowel cancer in 1993.

Alan Sealey scored the goals which gave West Ham United the European Cup-winners' Cup in 1965. He signed for the Hammers from Orient in 1961 and was almost a national hero after the game against TSV Munich. But a freak injury – he broke a leg playing cricket – saw him play only four more League games for West Ham. He had a brief spell with Plymouth, having scored 26 goals in 128 senior games for the Hammers. Alan Sealey died in 1996, aged only 53.

Skipper Bobby Moore and Olympiakos captain Polychroniou are in the arms of Russian referee Bachramov before the start of the European Cup-winners' match in Athens in December 1965. The Hammers reached the semi-final where they were knocked out by Borussia Dortmund. Referee Bachramov became famous seven months later when he was the linesman who gave Geoff Hurst's goal in the 1966 World Cup Final against West Germany.

Sir Geoff Hurst was just plain Geoff when he joined the Hammers in 1960. Six years later he was immortalised when he became the only man ever to score a hat-trick in a World Cup Final. Hurst made 499 senior appearances for West Ham (only one of them as a substitute) and scored 248 goals before moving to Stoke City for £80,000 in 1972. Forty-nine full caps brought him 24 goals altogether.

Remember him? It is April 1965 and new Hammers apprentice poses rather coyly for the camera. It is, of course, Trevor Brooking, who went on to become one of the greatest names in the club's history.

Jim Standen grabs the ball at Goodison Park in January 1966 as Everton's Derek Temple and Standen's teammate Martin Peters run in. The game ended 2-2.

Aston Villa goalkeeper Colin Withers can't stop Martin Peters' shot at Upton Park in March 1967. West Ham won 2-1.

West Ham's John Charles and Arsenal's Jimmy Robertson in action during the goalless draw at Highbury in October 1968.

Geoff Hurst hammers the ball through a crowded Derby County goalmouth at Upton Park in November 1969. Roy McFarland takes evasive action. The Hammers won 3-0. Former Spurs legend Dave Mackay is one of the Rams players looking on.

Jimmy Greaves marked his Hammers debut with two goals at Maine Road, where West Ham beat Manchester City 5-1 in March 1970. This is one of them, beating Tony Book and Ron Healy of City.

Jimmy Greaves is on the mark yet again, at Highbury on the last day of the 1969-70 season. Alas, the Hammers still went down 2-1.

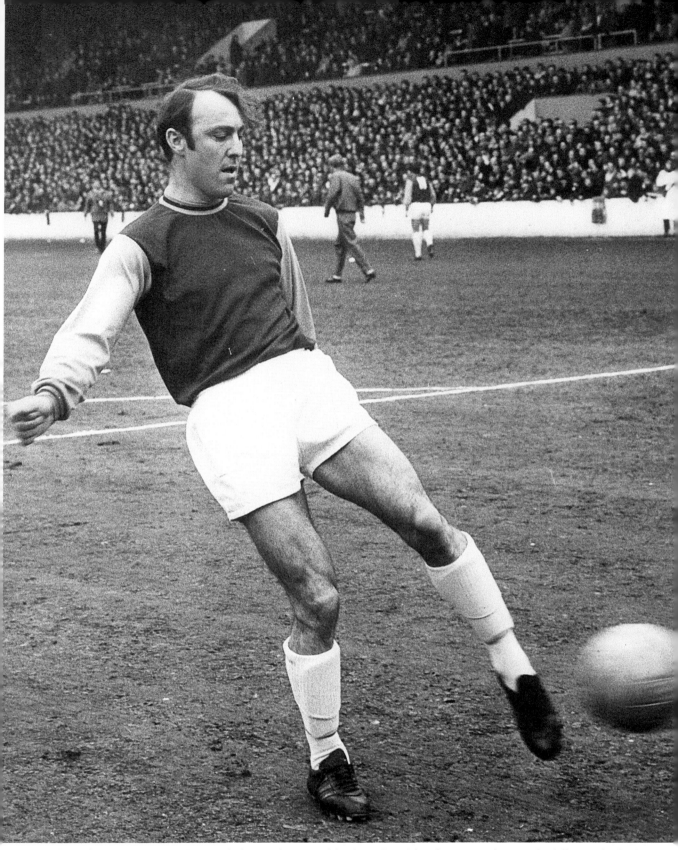

Jimmy Greaves was a goalscoring legend who netted on every debut he made – club and country, and at every level. He scored twice in his first game for West Ham, who he joined in 1970, for £200,00 in the deal which saw Martin Peters move in the opposite direction to White Hart Lane. Greaves scored 13 goals in 40 games for the Hammers. In his career he scored 357 First Division goals, 35 in the FA Cup and 44 in 57 full internationals for England. He started with Chelsea, went to Spurs via Italian football, and later overcame alcoholism to forge a career in broadcasting.

Chelsea's Peter
Osgood is left
trailing by Clyde
Best at Stamford
Bridge in December
1970. Chelsea won
2-1.

Brian Dear is the
subject of a tackle
from Chelsea's
David Webb.

Clyde Best beats Arsenal's Frank McLintock but heads over the Arsenal bar at Highbury in January 1971. The Hammers lost 2-0.

Manchester City's Francis Lee gets in a header at Upton Park in February 1971. Peter Eustace and Bobby Moore (6) are the Hammers players. The game ended 0-0.

Frank Lampard and Billy Bonds take on Derby's Kevin Hector and John McGovern at Upton Park in February 1971. The Rams won 4-2 to plunge the Hammers further into relegation trouble.

Ipswich Town's Jimmy Robertson slips the ball past West Ham's John McDowell at Upton Park in March 1971. The game ended 2-2 and at the end of the season the Hammers narrowly avoided the drop into Division Two.

Frank Lampard made 663 first-team appearances and scored 22 goals for the Hammers between 1967-68 and 1984-85. He signed as an apprentice and overcame a broken leg during his career. His two full caps for England came eight years apart. Lampard moved to Southend in 1985 and was later Harry Redknapp's assistant at Upton Park before both left in an acrimonious fall-out. His son, also Frank, also starred for the Hammers but left in the wake of his father's departure and signed for Chelsea.

Billy Bonds cost West Ham £50,000 when he signed from Charlton Athletic in 1967. He repaid that fee many times over and his 793 first-team appearances are a club record unlikely to be beaten. Bonds, who scored 59 goals from midfield, skippered the Hammers to two FA Cup Final victories and later took over as manager at Upton Park.

Bermuda-born striker Clyde Best scored 58 goals in 218 senior appearances for the Hammers after his debut in 1969-70. He left West Ham, his only League club, in 1976.

John Lyall served West Ham United for 34 years as office boy, player, coach and manager. Ilford-born, he joined the office staff in 1955, played in the FA Youth Cup Final in 1957 and was capped for England Youth and made his League debut in 1960. Injuries disrupted his playing career and after only 31 senior appearances he was forced to retire and return to office work. Lyall qualified as a coach under Ron Greenwood. In 1974 he was appointed team manager under Greenwood and when Greenwood became England boss, Lyall took over fully. Under him the Hammers twice won the FA Cup and finished third in the top flight, their highest-ever position. It was a shock when he was dismissed in 1989, in favour of Lou Macari.

Arsenal's Bob Wilson is the subject of a strong challenge from Geoff Hurst at Upton Park in December 1971. Peter Simpson appears to getting in his goalkeeper's way. Bob McNab (3) and Clyde Best watch and wait. The game ended goalless.

Hammers goalkeeper Mervyn Day was relieved to see this Manchester City effort rebound off a post to safety at Upton Park in December 1973.

Billy Bonds looks like a whirling dervish against Derby County at Upton Park in October 1973. The result was another 0-0 draw.

Mervyn Day kept goal for West Ham in 231 senior games. He signed as an apprentice in 1971 and moved to Orient in 1979 before returning to the top flight with Aston Villa.

Former Hammers star Martin Peters and West Ham's Kevin Lock both attempt to head the ball with their eyes shut at White Hart Lane in September 1974, when Tottenham won 2-1.

West Ham's Billy Jennings gets in a header at Highbury in October 1974. Eddie Kelly, Terry Macini and John Radford are the Arsenal players. The Gunners won 3-0.

West Ham visited Highbury twice in the 1974-75 season, winning 2-0 in an FA Cup quarter-final match there in March. Brian Kidd and the Hammers' Kevin Lock are both airborne. West Ham went on to win the Cup that year.

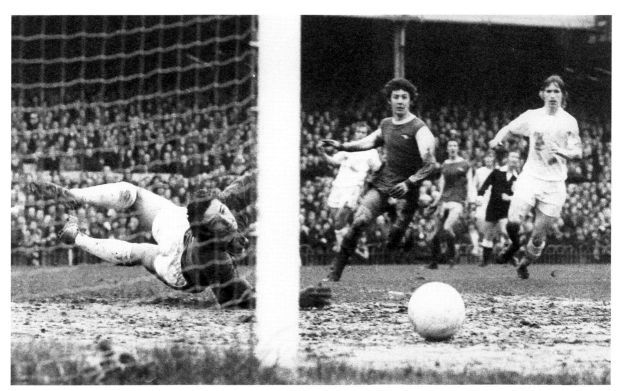

Mervyn Day makes a fine save from Arsenal's Brian Kidd in the FA Cup quarter-final match at Highbury in March 1975. Alan Taylor got both goals in West Ham's 2-0 win and they went on to beat Ipswich Town in a semi-final replay with Taylor again getting both goals.

West Ham line up for the camera before the 1975 FA Cup Final against Second Division Fulham. Back row (left to right): Bryan Robson, Clyde Best, Trevor Brooking, Bobby Ferguson, Mervyn Day, Kevin Lock, Pat Holland, John McDowell, Mick McGiven. Front row: Tommy Taylor, Keith Coleman, Bobby Gould, Frank Lampard, Alan Taylor, Graham Paddon, Billy Jennings.

Midfielder Pat Holland was unlucky with injuries throughout his career and it was injury which brought a premature end to his career in 1981, after 296 senior games and 32 goals. He joined the Hammers as an apprentice in 1968, turning professional the following year.

John McDowell was yet another local boy who joined the Hammers as an apprentice. He made 296 senior appearances between 1970-71 and 1978-79, after which he moved to Norwich City. Midway through his career he was affected by a bad knee injury.

Mervyn Day and Frank Lampard save the moment for the Hammers as Fulham's Les Barrett gets dangerously close to goal in the 1975 FA Cup Final. The Hammers won the Cup, 2-0, and yet again Alan Taylor scored both their goals.

Derby County's Roy McFarland hammers the ball into the Hammers' net during the FA Charity Shield match at Wembley on a scorching August afternoon in 1975. Derby, the League champions, won 2-0.

Alan Taylor became a household name when he helped West Ham win the FA Cup in 1975. He scored two goals in each of the quarter-final, semi-final and Wembley games. He joined the Hammers from Rochdale in 1974 and altogether scored 36 goals in 121 first-team games. In 1979, having struggled with injuries, he was transferred to Norwich City.

Trevor Brooking is a West Ham legend in his own lifetime. A total of 635 first-team appearances and 102 goals tells only part of the story. From signing as an apprentice in 1965 until he retired as a player in 1984, Brooking proved to be one of the most outstanding figures in football, not least for his gentlemanly approach to the game. Capped 47 times for England, Brooking is a successful businessman, a highly-respected media figure – and even found time to manage the club in 2003 after Glenn Roeder's illness.

Tommy Taylor joined West Ham from Orient for £80,000 in 1970 and was a regular at the centre of defence – he made 396 senior appearances – until he returned to Orient in 1979.

Alan Devonshire might have won more than eight England caps had he not suffered injury. He joined the Hammers in 1976, from non-League Southall, and went on to make 446 senior appearances, scoring 32 goals. He moved to Watford in 1990.

Bobby Ferguson made 276 appearances in goal for West Ham after joining them from Kilmarnock in 1967, for £65,000, then a British record for a 'keeper. Surprisingly, in his 13 years at Upton Park he never added to his seven Scotland caps. His last game for the club was in 1979-80 and he later emigrated to Australia.

Trevor Brooking slots the ball past Eintracht Frankfurt goalkeeper Peter Kunter on a rain-soaked night at Upton Park in April 1976 and the Hammers are on their way to another European Cup-winners' Cup Final. West Ham won the tie 4-3 on aggregate but lost the Final in Brussels, 4-2 to Anderlecht, the Belgian Cup holders.

Ups and Downs

Andy Gray scores the only goal of the League game between the Hammers and Aston Villa in January 1977. A week later the sides met again at Villa Park, where West Ham were knocked out of the FA Cup.

Billy Bonds is just too late to stop Andy Gray getting in a left-foot shot.

Alan Taylor takes the ball past Arsenal goalkeeper Jimmy Rimmer for one of his two goals in the Hammers' 3-2 win at Highbury in February 1977.

Alan Curbishley looks puffed as Arsenal's Frank McLintock bundles into him at Highbury in October 1977. The game ended in a 3-0 defeat for the Hammers who were relegated at the end of the season.

Mervyn Day is helpless as Ken McNaught opens the scoring for
Aston Villa at Upton Park in the 2-2 draw in October 1977.

Watford's Luther Blissett sends a diving header towards the West Ham goal as Hammers skipper Billy Bonds and Watford centre-forward
Ross Jenkins look on. Bryan Robson scored the only goal of this game in January 1978 as the Hammers moved into the fourth round of
the FA Cup, where they went out to QPR, 6-1 in a replay.

Bryan 'Pop' Robson scored 104 goals in 254 senior games for West Ham. He first signed for the Hammers in 1971, for a club record fee of £120,000 from Newcastle United. He moved to Sunderland in 1973-74 but returned for £80,000 in 1976. In 1979 he went back to Sunderland once more.

Aston Villa's Dennis Mortimer heads his side's third goal against West Ham at Villa Park in March 1978. The game ended 4-1 in Villa's favour.

Trevor Brooking is challenged by Gary Locke of Chelsea with the Blues' John Bumstead also close at hand. The Hammers lost this Second Division game 2-1 at Stamford Bridge in November 1979.

Centre-half Alvin Martin signed as an apprentice in 1974 and made 530 senior appearances, scoring 31 goals, before being given a free transfer in 1991-92. He was capped 17 times for England.

Steve Gritt of Charlton heads the ball past Hammers goalkeeper Phil Parkes for the only goal of the game at The Valley in December 1979.

Frank Lampard and Liam Brady of Arsenal go tumbling at Wembley in the 1980 FA Cup Final.

Paul Allen became the youngest player ever to appear in an FA Cup Final when he helped the Hammers beat Arsenal in the 1980 Wembley game when he was only 17. In 1985, after 196 senior games for West Ham, he joined his cousin Clive Allen at Spurs. Clive's father, Les, had been a big favourite at White Hart Lane in the 1950s.

David O'Leary hammers the ball clear from a West Ham United attack in the 1980 FA Cup Final.

One of the most famous goals in West Ham's history. Trevor Brookings gets in a rare header and wins the FA Cup for the Hammers.

Happy Hammers! West Ham players parade the FA Cup around Wembley.

Goalkeeper Phil Parkes made 436 senior appearances for the Hammers after signing for the club in February 1979, from QPR for £525,000, then the highest fee ever paid for a British goalkeeper. It was John Lyall who signed Parkes for West Ham and it was Lyall who took him to Ipswich Town in 1990. Parkes, who was capped once for England, made 344 League appearances for the Hammers, exactly the same total for QPR, and when his appearances for Walsall, his first club, are added in, he appeared in over 700 League games in his career.

ND - #0374 - 270225 - C0 - 260/195/8 - PB - 9781780911359 - Gloss Lamination